Original title:
A Jungle in a Pot

Copyright © 2025 Creative Arts Management OÜ
All rights reserved.

Author: Alec Davenport
ISBN HARDBACK: 978-1-80581-928-8
ISBN PAPERBACK: 978-1-80581-455-9
ISBN EBOOK: 978-1-80581-928-8

Tranquil Traces of Life

In a little bowl so round,
Tiny critters can be found,
A squirrel dons a tiny hat,
While a beetle dances, just like that.

An ant in boots begins to prance,
And grasshoppers join for a chance,
They gather round for a grand feast,
Nibbling crumbs, oh what a beast!

A catnip plant, the main stage set,
Where every creature finds their pet,
A worm plays king, a leaf his throne,
They laugh and cheer, they're never alone.

The sky above is just a lamp,
And fireflies glow like a stamp,
In the wild world of potted fun,
Life is short, so let's just run!

Foliage in a Container

A cactus wearing sunglasses, bright and bold,
Sips on water, cool and controlled.
A vine climbs high on a shelf made of wood,
Mimicking a climber, oh, how it would!

Tiny flowers dancing, a cheeky parade,
In pots they conspire, mischief is made.
Moss in the corners, with secrets to share,
Their whispers of laughter float through the air.

Verdant Dreams in Clay

A fern checks its pulse, quite the dramatic flair,
While the soil giggles and tosses its hair.
A geranium grins, in polka-dot socks,
Swaying with frogs, they're friends 'round the rocks.

The pot winks slyly, a true little tease,
While sprouts tell tall tales of globe-trotting bees.
In the box of mud, where the wild ones hide,
Laughter erupts with the tiniest pride.

Urban Greenery's Whisper

In a tin can garden, the herbs start to chat,
A basil sings operas, and mint tips his hat.
While sprouts share their gossip, over a brew,
"Lettuce be friends," they croon, quite the crew!

A tomato in overalls struts with tough grace,
Flashing a smile, oh what a bold face!
Each leaf takes a bow to the sunny binge,
As laughter erupts from the tallest fringe.

Terra Cotta Oasis

In earthy vessels, the plants throw a rave,
With rhythms of roots, they dance and they wave.
A potted palm prances, in its leafy attire,
While succulents join in, igniting the fire.

A daisy decides to wear polka-dot style,
A sunbeam contests who can shine with more smile.
The soil hums tunes of life's vibrant jest,
In this charming patch, it's simply the best!

The Hidden Canopy

In a tin can, a tree does grow,
A tiny forest, don't you know?
Squirrels made of plastic play,
In this pot, they laugh and sway.

Mossy carpets, oh what a sight,
Fuzzy creatures in the night.
Little birds sing a tune,
While a gnome juggles with a spoon.

Gardener's Delights in Microcosm

In a cup, a garden blooms,
With cacti spiking all the rooms.
A worm in sunglasses has a dream,
To find a puddle for a swim team.

Bees made of feathers buzz around,
A micro world so profound.
The sun smiles when the raindrops dance,
While ants in tuxedos steal a glance.

Echoes of Wilderness in Stillness

A rabbit hops on plastic grass,
Wonders if the dogs will pass.
Giraffes poke their heads quite high,
Chasing clouds that float and sigh.

A parrot speaks in silly rhymes,
Discussing love in garden times.
The pots around join in the chat,
While frogs pretend to be quite fat.

Terracotta Tales of Wonder

In the clay, a tale unfolds,
Of adventurers brave and bold.
A tortoise wearing shoes of red,
Shares secrets that he has read.

The daisies plot a funny show,
As a banana tree sways slow.
Jars of jellybeans parade,
While crickets chirp a serenade.

A Symphony in Green

Tiny leaves dance in the breeze,
Whispers of secrets among the trees.
A puppet show of twirling vines,
As garden gnomes sip elderflower wines.

Squirrels wear hats in a stylish flair,
While raccoons debate without a care.
Chirping frogs sing an offbeat tune,
In this lively plot, under the moon.

Worms throw raves at the root's deep end,
While ants are busy in their blend.
With a splash of soil and a dash of sun,
This vibrant shindig has just begun!

In this world of green and joy,
Every plant's a quirky ploy.
Who knew a pot could hold such fun,
With laughter blooming, never done!

Garden of the Mind

In a pot where ideas sprout,
Thoughts twirl and spin about.
The daisies hum a curious tune,
While cacti dance with a rattling swoon.

Pansies giggle at the jokes we share,
While snapdragons lend a careful glare.
Ivy climbs high, seeking some fame,
In our playful plot, it's all a game!

Mushrooms wear hats to play pretend,
As tumbleweeds roll, the fun won't end.
With sunbeams coaxing treasures to bloom,
Imagination scatters all the gloom.

In this mental realm, we sip our tea,
With laughter floating like a bumblebee.
No rules to bind, just joyous delight,
In our mind's garden, everything feels right!

The Secret Garden's Embrace

Behind the leaves, laughter hides,
With whispers of joy on the breezy tides.
A hidden world of fun unfolds,
As playful petals share their tales bold.

The lavender tickles the bees' funny bone,
While dandelions laugh, never alone.
In this secret haven, gnomes play chess,
As laughter echoes, the day's a success!

Beetles don capes in a sprightly race,
As butterflies can't keep a steady pace.
Potted wonders, lively and bright,
In this cozy nook, everything feels right!

With sunshine paints splashed on the walls,
And giggling leaves when the wind calls.
Even the soil can crack a grin,
In this embrace, joy dances within!

Petals and Pottery

Sunflowers gaze from their clay throne,
While tulips whisper secrets, not alone.
In this art of soil and sprout,
Every blossom knows what it's about.

Ceramic frogs sport stylish hats,
While busy bees joke with the chitchats.
Pots filled with stories and brilliant sights,
Creating smiles on sunny nights.

Lily pads float with a ballet grace,
As clay figures join in the race.
With each twist and turn, the colors sing,
In this pottery world, joy's the king!

So come and dance in this vibrant fest,
With petals and pots, we are truly blessed.
Nature's laughter painted with flair,
In a garden where joy hangs in the air!

Chromatic Canopy

In a ceramic land, colors bloom,
Leaves dance like socks in a crowded room.
Tiny vines climb to the sky, oh my!
A parrot squawks just to catch our eye.

Each petal's a wink, a secret tease,
Tickling the air, like a summer breeze.
A daisy giggles, a fern starts to sway,
Who knew plants could have so much to say?

Dappled Light of Home

Sunbeams poke through like little spies,
Tickling the leaves, oh how they rise!
A cheeky cactus wearing a crown,
Pretending to be the king of the town.

The soil's a stage for jokesters to play,
Worms wriggle by in a comical way.
With every sprout, a joke unfolds,
Nature's punchlines in greens and golds.

Vessel of Secrets

Inside the pot, a comedy act,
Sassy ferns make bold contact.
Flowers gossip, they whisper and share,
As tiny bugs pull up a chair.

A tulip claims it's the belle of the ball,
While succulents play football, not caring at all.
This little world, so lively and bright,
Turns every morning into a delight.

The Pot's Heartbeat

The pot beats like a silly drum,
With every drop, it goes 'thump-thump-thrum.'
Roots tap dance in a cozy retreat,
While raindrops giggle at their own beat.

A leafy chorus sings in the shade,
With playful shadows that never fade.
In this tiny realm, laughter's the key,
Each pot's a party—come join, oh me!

Potent Flora Fantasia

In the corner, plants reside,
A leafy crew, full of pride.
Cacti in hats, so fancy and bright,
Giggling away in the morning light.

Petunias in shades of vibrant hue,
Throw parties when no one is due.
Dancing with sunlight, they form a chain,
Each petal's a story, quite hard to explain.

A fern in a corner, stretching its limbs,
Almost a gymnast, performing with whims.
Succulents mumble in soft, silly tones,
Mysteries whispered in green, leafy groans.

Together they thrive in this tiny domain,
A riot of colors, some laughter, some rain.
With roots intertwined, they hold on tight,
To the joy of their world, oh what a sight!

Echoes of the Rainforest

In a pot where the green things hum,
A little world where the wild ones come.
Bamboo shoots clatter, gossip aflight,
Sharing secrets in the soft daylight.

The violets giggle, as petals unfold,
Telling tales of adventures bold.
One leaf claims it's danced with the breeze,
While the herbs all chuckle with teasing ease.

A tiny fern dons a crown made of dust,
Proclaiming itself the king, so just!
Together they plot for a grand escape,
To discover what's beyond the pot's shape.

With twirls and sways, they make quite the show,
In leafy cabarets, where laughter does grow.
A salute from the soil, a wink from the sun,
In this whimsical haven, fun's never done!

Lush Sanctuary

There's a kingdom nestled on the sill,
With tiny monarchs making a thrill.
Tiny vines wrestling in good-natured fights,
While daisies whirl in their floral delights.

A roguish cactus brandishes its spikes,
Telling wild tales of adventures on hikes.
A marigold chuckles, recounts a prank,
As the others nod, giving thanks from their tank.

The herbs gather round for a seasonal feast,
While petunias recite poems, at least.
Moss makes a hat for the shadows to wear,
In this pot of laughter, there's joy in the air.

Beneath the soil, the roots start to dance,
Each sprout with a little, green, twinkling glance.
In this cozy abode where flora unite,
They create a fun fest, oh what a sight!

A Symphony of Leaves

In a kaleidoscope of green and gold,
The plants strike up a tune, oh so bold.
A choir of leaves sings sweetly at dawn,
With melodies floating, like a frolicsome fawn.

The daisies sway, in a delicate trance,
While thorns from the roses just want to dance.
Chasing each other in playful delight,
Creating a symphony, oh what a sight!

A wandering petal whispers a joke,
To the herbaceous crowd, they giggle and poke.
A giggling green world with stories to share,
Where laughter erupts in the warm, sunny air.

Together they thrive in verdant embrace,
In a pot full of joy, they've found their own space.
With banter and giggles, they grow side by side,
In this leafy ensemble, where fun won't subside!

A Captive Leaf

In a tiny container, a leaf took a stand,
Waving its arms like a rock band.
It danced on its stem, a comedic sight,
Shouting, 'I'm the king of this leafy delight!'

The soil whispered jokes, it giggled with glee,
While a raindrop slid by, shouting, 'Look at me!'
A sunbeam chimed in, with a warm little pun,
'Life's a pot party, and we're all having fun!'

The pest, a bold aphid, tried to wage war,
But the leaf just laughed, 'I'm too cute to pour!'
With a flick and a flap, it sent them all flying,
Said, 'Please do return, I've been so accommodating!'

So in this small garden, all creatures unite,
Creating their joy in the dim kitchen light.
With a chuckle and grin, they flourish anew,
In their captive abode, where the laughter just grew!

Lush Dreams in Terra

Within this deep pot, what wonders unfold,
A green thumb's treasure, a story retold.
Ferns dance like dancers, with fronds all a-flutter,
While cacti compare their spikes over butter.

An onion starts crying, 'I'm just too emotional!'
While the basil retorts, 'You're simply promotional!'
The mint rolls its leaves, snags an adoring glance,
Saying, 'I'm the one who'll lead the herb dance!'

While shadows giggle, the sun beams reveal,
That roots share their tales with each twist and each squeal.
As worms pass the gossip beneath the soil bed,
They cackle, 'We've never been bored here!' instead.

So take a look down, this pot wears a crown,
In the court of the greens, there's no chance of frown.
With personalities sprouting, it's safe to presume,
This jungle of joy makes a magical room!

Pint-Sized Paradise

In a cup so small, a jungle takes flight,
With tiny green warriors, ready to fight.
A sprout waves a flag, 'No space can contain!'
Boundless adventures in this tiny domain!

The ivy climbs high, like it's craving some fame,
While thyme starts a band, calling out each name.
'We'll tour the kitchen, spread laughter and cheer,
Who needs a vast world? We've plenty right here!'

A ladybug giggles, believes it's a queen,
While a rogue little snail claims a throne in between.
They laugh at the cat, who's towering and grand,
'This pot is our kingdom, we rule the land!'

So join in the fun, let your worries all cease,
In a pint-sized paradise, you'll find your peace.
With greens on the rise, and laughter on call,
Together we sing, 'There's joy for us all!'

Color and Chaos

In a tiny pot, mayhem blooms bright,
Colors collide like a paintball fight.
The peas pull pranks, the carrots all cheer,
While the radish yells, 'Hey, come join us here!'

Tangled vines laugh as they wiggle and sway,
'Up here in the chaos, we party all day!'
Bright flowers compete for the sun's warm embrace,
Saying, 'I'm the prettiest in this crowded space!'

Bugs turn the drama into a grand play,
Flying around like they own the main stage.
The earthworms cheer, 'We've got jokes for days!'
This tangled-up dance, a wild, funny maze!

So behold this mess, where laughter's a must,
In chaos, we flourish, together we rust.
A riot of color feeds our carefree dreams,
In this pot full of laughter, we're bursting at the seams!

Whims of the Wilderness

In a corner, plants collide,
A cactus and fern, side by side.
The fern keeps whispering, "Look at me!"
While the cactus just rolls in glee.

A spider spins a strange ballet,
While the violets just plan their stay.
"Watch out! Here comes a cheeky ant!"
"Don't worry! He's just here to plant!"

Arbor in Abeyance

A leafy friend in a pot does sway,
Telling stories of a sunny day.
Its roots in mischief, a dance they start,
While tiny hands try to take their part.

A squirrel peeked in, what a surprise!
Finding treasures beneath the skies.
"This is my turf!" the plant did shout,
But the squirrel just laughed, wriggled about.

World of Whimsy

In a tiny pot, a world is born,
A dandelion dreams of being adorned.
"I'm a giant!" it shouts with pride,
While a little snail decides to slide.

The daisies giggle, swaying low,
As the soil swirls in a funny show.
"I'll be a tree!" a sprout proclaimed,
But the others just chuckled, unashamed.

The Microcosmic Garden

In a bright pot, the excitement grows,
Each tiny leaf, a tale it shows.
The basil winks with a spicy grin,
While the thyme just rolls when it's in a spin.

A ladybug lands, what a parade!
Dancing atop the green cascade.
"I'm the queen!" she chirps with flair,
While the mint just sighs, tossing hair.

Exotic Fragments

Tiny leaves peep out from the rim,
Hoping to bask in a sunbeam's whim.
A tiny monkey swings by with glee,
In this pot, they think it's a tree!

A tortoise strolls, taking its time,
Hoping to mimic a muddy climb.
The soil whispers secrets to each sprout,
Where have the squirrels wandered out?

Gnomes in shades cheer on the scene,
They wave their flags, a leafy green.
With every raindrop, they have a feast,
A banquet fit for a plant-based beast!

Underneath this cozy shell,
All our friends plot and dwell.
In this world of miniatures quite absurd,
A garden fizzles, alive and stirred.

Enclosed Eden

Inside a pot, the magic swells,
Where herbs play games and nature dwells.
Tomatoes start a dance-off show,
While basil shimmies, putting on a glow.

Caterpillars cheer with a munching sound,
As ladybugs twirl all around.
Chives sing songs both high and low,
In this little patch, the fun will flow.

But then a cat leaps for a taste,
Creating chaos, oh what a haste!
Plants scatter, they scurry and dart,
In this leafy world, it's quite an art!

Yet through the shambles, joy remains,
In the tiniest pot, life entertains.
With laughter echoing in each leaf,
This pot of wonders, beyond belief.

Ferns and Fernweh

With wispy fronds that sway and sway,
Ferns dream of forests far away.
Yet here they grow in fluff and mud,
Wondering, 'Is this all, or should we flood?'

A squirrel in a raincoat bumbles by,
Complaining, 'It's too small, oh why?
I need a jungle, or at least a tree,
Not just this pot, can't you see?'

But vines giggle, twisting with flair,
'This is our world, we love it here!'
The pot may be small, but the joy is grand,
In this little realm, dreams aren't banned.

And so they bask in their cozy space,
Where moss grows soft, an emerald lace.
Every plant is a friend, wild and free,
In their mini realm, they're all they can be!

The Captive Canopy

In a pot, where shadows play,
A little tree dreams of the bay.
It sways and creaks, with tales to spin,
Of adventures in jungles, its woven kin.

A frog with a crown croaks loud and proud,
Claiming his throne in the leafy crowd.
Lizards play hide and seek with the thyme,
While a snail does a slow-motion climb.

But thunder sounds like a booming joke,
As rain falls down—a plant friend poke!
Leaves flap wildly, giggling with cheer,
In this glorious pot, joy's always near.

Though confined to a rim, they laugh and grow,
Imagining wild, with each little show.
Their hearts are free, and so they cope,
In this colorful band, there's always hope!

The Wildness at My Feet

In a tiny pot, I spy,
A fierce green beast, oh my!
A feral fern, with leaves so steep,
Watch your toes, it likes to creep!

A bustling bud, all sprout and flare,
It stole my sunshine, I swear!
With roots that wiggle like a worm,
Life here has quite the wild term!

A tiny vine climbs so high,
Reaching up for the sky.
I chop them back, but they don't care,
Tomorrow they'll be everywhere!

With laughter ringing through the night,
In this small world, there's no fright.
Nature's capers are taking flight,
In my pot, I find delight!

Miniature Wilderness

In a bowl, both round and bright,
A scene unfolds, what a sight!
A cactus trying to start a fight,
"Don't touch my water, it's my right!"

A tiny tree with branches thick,
Sways to wind, a jolly trick.
Leaves that dance, they glow and shine,
Potted wonder with a twist of vine.

A cheeky flower, yellow and bold,
Spills its secrets, stories told.
"Here's my nectar, come take a sip!"
All my ants now run and skip!

Smaller beasts than in the wild,
Each one spry, each one wild.
In this little world, life runs free,
Who needs the woods? Just look at me!

Potted Lushness

In this pot, there's no restraint,
A leafy dictator with no complaint.
With each new sprout, it takes its stand,
Declaring war on our kitchen land!

A marigold, with quite the flair,
Says "I can grow anywhere!"
Sticks its tongue out at the sun,
In this pot, it's having fun!

A mossy mat, a sneaky trick,
Quietly growing, oh so slick.
Whispers to the roots below,
"Let's prank the beans, they'll never know!"

With pots that giggle and plants that sway,
The silliness blooms in a fabulous way.
In this garden, the laughter won't stop,
Making a fuss in a tiny crop!

The Enchanted Blossom Box

In this box, a plant parade,
Marigolds marching, unafraid.
Tulips twirling in a show,
It's a party down below!

Basil's wearing a chef's hat tight,
Mint is dancing, what a sight!
Chives are singing, crisp and green,
The funniest show you've ever seen!

Daisies gossip, petals wide,
Cacti stand with prickly pride.
Each bloom whispers a silly tune,
All this happens beneath the moon!

In this box, a circus grows,
Where every leaf has a nose.
Laughs erupt from silly roots,
In my garden, joy reboots!

Secrets of Growth in Silence

In a tiny world, plants wear their hats,
Cacti do a tango, oh, imagine that!
While ferns gossip secrets, low in the shade,
And the herbs trade jokes that never quite fade.

The pots are all crowded, but oh what a sight,
A tiny green jungle, a pure delight.
Every leaf's a warrior, lush and robust,
In this silent circus, laughter is a must!

Shhh, listen close, can you hear the plants?
Doing their best in dance-like prants.
Their roots talk in whispers, oh, what a tale,
Of growing in quiet, without any fail.

In this kingdom of green, they play hide-and-seek,
With soil their kingdom, it's fun, not bleak.
They giggle in sunlight, dance to the rain,
In this little world, it's all joy, no pain.

The Lush Room Adventure

Once in a room where the greenery thrived,
The rubber plant lost and the ivy arrived.
Chasing a spider with eight tiny legs,
While ferns whisper loudly at neighboring pegs.

A cactus called Barry cracked up at a joke,
About a lazy bean whose sprouts seldom woke.
The marigolds laughed, in loud, vibrant hues,
As the pot plants debated on which drink to choose.

They hosted a party with candles of light,
Each leaf donned a cap, oh, what a sight!
With snacks made of sunshine and fresh morning dew,
The friends all gathered, it was quite the brew!

Silly tales sprouted as they swayed in the breeze,
"Did you hear about Bob? He grew in two peas!"
The laughter erupted, a glorious cheer,
In this little room, there's nothing to fear!

Whispers of the Green Abyss

Betwixt pots and soils, small secrets convene,
In shadows of leaves, they plot and they scheme.
A bamboo declares, 'I'll stretch to the sky!'
While succulents snicker at grass going dry.

"Who's the tallest?" a thyme plant did pose,
With a wink, the basil flaunted her rose.
The mint took a bow, in her vibrant attire,
While the ivy climbed higher, fueled by desire.

"Let's race to the window, quick as can be!"
A sweet, daring challenge from the great rubber tree.
They swished and they swayed in a lively parade,
With roots intertwined, it was all a charade.

In echoes of laughter, they flourish with glee,
As the world outside buzzes, not for them, see?
The green whispers tales of a world so wide,
Yet happy they are, with each other, they bide.

Secrets Beneath the Soil

Under the surface where few dare to peek,
Roots twist in a tango, so playful, so sleek.
The worms throw a party, their music quite wild,
As they groove in the dark, nature's joyful child.

"I'm growing a treasure!" exclaimed a young sprout,
While the potatoes agreed, "There's no fear about!"
They chuckle and jest while the soil's in a dance,
In their earthy domain, they all take a chance.

A radish confided, "I'd like some more sun!"
While carrots just chuckled, "We're fine, we just run!"
They shared silly stories, how leaves outshine roots,
And giggles erupted—what fun in their boots!

So if you look down, beneath layers of brown,
You'll find a grand saga, no chance of a frown.
In the soil, there's laughter, a carnival show,
Trust that the whispers of green often flow!

Guardians of Green

In a little pot, plants loom high,
With rubbery leaves that seem to sigh.
A cactus is pranking an old fern,
While the basil whispers, 'Wait your turn!'

In the corner, a sneaky sprout,
Tries to wiggle, tries to shout.
Potting soil goes flying wide,
As petals blush from all the pride.

A tiny spider spins a plot,
To sneak some sun—oh, clever thought!
The daisies giggle, their heads held tall,
While parsley dreams of a garden ball.

Little guardians, green and bright,
Dancing shadows in morning light.
Each day's a party in the mix,
With nature's charm and lots of tricks!

Enigmatic Growth

In a bowl so small, a mystery brews,
It's hard to tell what will sprout and choose.
A bean plant's got its head in the clouds,
While thyme just giggles behind its shrouds.

Tomato's a joker, wearing a frown,
Sneaking on ginger trying to clown.
The ivy's plotting a daring scheme,
To take the stage and upend the dream.

A rhubarb thinks it's a pop star tonight,
Singing to sage in the warm moonlight.
Lettuce laughs, saying, "What a show!"
While spinach rolls in, stealing the glow.

In this wild pot, secrets unfurl,
Each plant a player in the green swirl.
Who knew such chaos could bloom in delight?
With whimsical wonders, the stars shine bright!

Nature's Nucleus

In a pot where laughter sprigs,
Tiny roots do little jigs.
A mint leaves giggle, quite a tease,
While sage is swaying in the breeze.

The soil is rich with silly dreams,
Carrots conspire with radish schemes.
Chives hold court with their regal flair,
While thyme and basil play musical chairs.

Pots spin tales of airborne leaps,
And daisies whisper all their peeps.
A sprout's ambition? Rise to the top,
While the broccoli quips, "Here I'll stop!"

In this lively cradle, joy's amiss,
All nature's creatures can't help but kiss.
As the sun shines down, and shadows flirt,
The nucleus blooms in this playful dirt!

Abundant Awakening

In a cheerful pot, where wonders sprout,
Tiny new friends begin to shout.
With radishes forming quirky lines,
And parsley flipping its fancy twines.

The peas are plotting a daring game,
While bean shoots show off their silly fame.
"Oh watch me grow!" one proudly boasts,
As mushrooms giggle, "We're the hosts!"

Lettuce lounges, reclined and free,
While marigolds dance with glee.
A vibrant mix of colors bright,
Creating chaos, pure delight.

In this cozy pot, laughter swells,
As herbs share tales with vibrant knells.
Abundant joy in each little sprout,
As nature's party roars about!

Ethereal Foliage Dreams

In a tiny realm where plants conspire,
A cactus dances with a burst of fire.
The ferns wear hats, all fresh and bright,
While peas in pods join the leafy fright.

The snails wear boots, slick and neat,
Jiving to the rhythm, their little feet.
A spider weaves tales from a thread so fine,
Making merry tunes with a twirl and twine.

Above, a ladybug holds court with glee,
Telling tall stories of the old oak tree.
The grasshoppers laugh as they hop all around,
Creating a circus, with joy abound.

Lilies in laughter, a riotous bunch,
Spilling their secrets over a crunchy lunch.
In this whimsical place where humor flows,
Nature's own comedy garden grows!

The Secret Grotto

In a wee corner where shadows play,
Lurks a broccoli monster, frosty and gray.
It guards all the carrots with a cautious gaze,
While peas roll by in a frolicsome daze.

Beetles croon ballads, strumming on leaves,
As the radishes giggle, the lively thieves.
Mushrooms tiptoe, in vibrant attire,
Throwing wild parties that never tire.

The tomatoes plot in crimson hues,
Creating hilarity in their own little ruse.
A leek plays the flute, with style and flair,
While beans climb high, beyond compare.

In this grotto of secrets, all so absurd,
Funny tales unravel with every word.
Every leaf whispers a joke that sways,
In this merry circus of potent displays!

Green Perceptions

In a cup of soil where the seeds all chat,
A dandelion sports a fancy hat.
The mint sprigs gossip in a minty swirl,
As thyme juggles herbs with a dainty twirl.

A beetroot boasts of its shiny skin,
While sprouts caper around in a spin.
Hilarity sprouts from the garden's core,
As worms tell tales about things that soar.

The sunbeams wink at the vibrant view,
While greens plot mischief with a laughing crew.
Basil's silly dance makes everyone cheer,
Potting humor and joy, it's the best time of year!

In this verdant world, laughter's the key,
With every petal, a chuckle promised free.
Nature's antics, a proper delight,
Sprouting smiles from morning till night!

Recesses of Nature

In a tiny world where the carrots roam,
A radish is king, in leafy chrome.
Shimmering sprouts in the sun's warm glow,
Joking with snails about the pace they go.

A mischievous beetle slips on a leaf,
While the daisies exchange tales of disbelief.
A wandering gnome with a jingly gait,
Joins the fun with a laugh that's first-rate.

Chickweed and clovers play hide and seek,
While the vine entertains with a wobbly streak.
The sun smiles down, in a golden tinge,
Painting giggles that seem to fringe.

Laughter sprouts from the roots of their game,
In the recess of greens, no two are the same.
This playful escape, where humor grows,
In nature's domain, where the funny flows!

Flora's Fable

In a bowl of green, a leaf does dance,
Tiny critters think they've found romance.
A squirrel scouts out a snack or two,
While a ladybug dreams of starting a zoo.

An ant holds court on a mossy throne,
Sharing tales of how he likes to groan.
Basil debates with the thyme in charge,
While sage mixes in its extra-large.

Sunlight spills over in golden glee,
Frogs croak gossip from the old pine tree.
With each drop of rain, a party begins,
Colors burst forth, let the fun commence!

So grab your cup of tea, sit right here,
In this hectic green, we've nothing to fear.
Laughter and growth with each passing hour,
In Flora's realm, there's never a sour.

The Tiny Thicket

A pot of gold, or so it seems,
Tiny plants organizing crazy dreams.
Lizards play tag while the soil rolls,
And worms compose tunes from underground holes.

A flower whispers secrets of the day,
While busy bees buzz in a sweet ballet.
Grasshoppers dance like they own the place,
While snippets of laughter fill every space.

With each twist and turn, calamities brew,
Vines wrestle to see who's the best at blue.
Cacti throw parties with prickly fun,
Everyone's invited; tonight, we run!

In this teacup jungle, life's never bland,
As each playful creature lends a helping hand.
So raise a little toast; let's cheer away,
To the tiny thicket, where we all play!

Vessels of Vitality

Within these walls, a riotous spree,
Chasing each other, crazy as can be.
A pot of laughter, the joy runs high,
Snakes slither past, saying, "Oh my, oh my!"

Moss forms pillows for naps in the day,
While seedlings gossip and giggle away.
Chirping crickets lead a raucous choir,
Tickling the air with their love of fire.

Cactus throws shade with a prickly grin,
As the succulents chuckle in the din.
With each little breeze, they wiggle and sway,
These vessels of life enjoy the ballet.

No need for a gardener in this fiesta,
Each leaf throws a party, such a fiesta!
So pour out the fun; let the good times roll,
In the colorful whirl of the plant-loving soul!

Rhythms of Rainy Days

Pitter-patter, the raindrops play,
Each little dribble's its own cabaret.
A pot of smiles with mud on the street,
Where the plants stomp along in a groovy beat.

Worms take to dancing in puddles so bold,
While spiders showcase their webs of gold.
Raindrops give rhythm to the frogs in the know,
And the sleepy sunflowers sway, stealing the show.

With every flash of lightning, a giggle erupts,
As beetles join in, skipping, leaping, and thumps.
Together they laugh, turning gloom into grace,
Transforming each drop into a party place.

So here's to the joy that rain can bestow,
In our leafy dwellings, come join the flow!
With a splash and a giggle, let's dance all day,
To the rhythms of rain that invite us to play!

Petal-Sparked Fantasies

In a vase, the plants play hide-and-seek,
Roots are too shy, they rarely speak.
Leaves wave like flags in a parade,
While thoughts of sunlight keep them swayed.

A sprout with dreams to climb the wall,
Whispers to a shelf, "I've got it all!"
Tiny flowers laugh when they bloom,
Worn-out jokes fill the living room.

A pot so round, it rolls in glee,
Claiming the title, "I am so free!"
Marigolds dance, they twist and twine,
Making their own version of fine wine.

At night, the globes of light appear,
Listening closely, you might hear cheer.
Garden gnomes join in for a spree,
Living it up—just like you and me!

The Outdated Orchard

In a corner, the fruit trees sigh,
Time to ripen? Oh my, oh my!
Bananas wrinkle, apples play coy,
A peach complained, "I lost my joy!"

With roots stuck fast in yesterday's soil,
Each fruit dreams of a life of toil.
Water drips down like laughter's stream,
While daisies wonder, "Is this a dream?"

The citrus burst, with zest and flair,
Squeezed lemons moaned, "Life's not fair!"
Cherry trees gossip about the bugs,
Debating who's the juiciest for hugs.

But here come the squirrels, quick and sly,
On high-speed chases, oh my, oh my!
Dancing under the moon's bright light,
Their nutty antics are pure delight!

Wonders in the Clay Realm

In a pot of clay, the wonders frolic,
Mischievous roots, they're so symbolic!
Worms play tag, zipping through the earth,
Each squishy twist reveals new worth.

A sprout with gossip, whispers soft,
While mossy friends hoot and scoff.
Caterpillars dress in colors bright,
Saying, "We're the stars of the night!"

Tiny raindrops dance on leaves,
While just below, the soil weaves.
A patchwork quilt of nature's cheer,
Tickling toes, reminding us here.

Sunshine's laughter fills every nook,
In this realm, not one is a rook.
They play their games, no need for rules,
The clay is home to silly jewels!

The Enclosure's Secret Life

Within clear walls, excitement brews,
Where busy critters trade their views.
A ladybug bakes under the sun,
As neighbors plot their next big fun.

Snails write letters, slimy and bold,
Tales of mischief, hardly told.
Lilies gossip, swaying with ease,
"Have you heard? The sun's a tease!"

In a tiny world, the laughter swings,
Every leaf tells of secret flings.
Mice wear hats made of grass, oh dear!
They toast to the moon with a cheer!

Each night they gather, a potluck grand,
With cookie crumbs sown from a small hand.
Beneath the stars, they sing their tune,
A quirky life in the afternoon!

Leafy Keep

In a tiny home, plants play hide and seek,
The foliage giggles, it's so unique.
Ferns do a dance, while cacti just prick,
A gnome shakes his head, thinking it's a trick.

A squirrel takes charge, setting the rules,
"Your leaves are too big for my tiny schools!"
The plants roll their eyes, they'll break all the norms,
In this leafy keep, chaos transforms.

Botanicals in a Bowl

In a grand ceramic, they twist and they twine,
Succulents grumble, "I wish I could shine!"
A spider plant laughs, "Just wait for the sun,
Soon all your colors will surely outrun."

An eager fern asks, "Who gets to be tall?"
"I'll stake my claim!" says the tiny pea doll.
They squabble and rumble, no roots to restrict,
In their whims and fancies, it's perfectly absurd.

The Enchanted Planter

In a pot of delight, where mischief abounds,
The violets plot giggles on soft, leafy mounds.
Basil likes gossip, thyme joins the fun,
While mint pulls a prank, watch out, here it comes!

With whispers of magic, they twist and they turn,
Each splash of green tells stories to learn.
A ladybug sings as she twirls in the air,
In this enchanted container, nothing is rare.

Emerald Oasis

In a bowl of green, where dreams take a flight,
The peas do a jig, full of delight.
The pots talk in whispers, sharing their glee,
While orchids roll their eyes, "Oh, let's all be free!"

With a splash of imagination, they wiggle with cheer,
Tales of adventure, both far and near.
In this emerald space, laughter and fun,
Each plant plays its part, under the sun.

Ferns & Fractals

In a tiny green space, ferns are spry,
Leaves twist and turn, reaching for the sky.
A fractal dance of shapes galore,
Who knew they'd grow in my kitchen floor?

Tiny bugs try to stage a parade,
Pushing their luck, they seem unafraid.
They hike on moss like it's a grand trip,
But I'm here, ready with a swift zip!

Roots intertwine like a tangled yarn,
Each morning feels like a plant-filled charm.
The herbs are plotting, nothing is meek,
A basil brigade on a leafy peak!

In pots they thrive, quite the sly crew,
Sprouting ideas, oh what shall we brew?
With laughter and whimsy, this greenish lot,
Turns all my worries into a pot!

Tranquil Leafy Haven

A cozy corner, where green friends convene,
Whispering secrets, oh what could they mean?
A rubber plant giggles, shaking with glee,
It knows all the dirt—spills it on me!

Pothos vines twirling in a sly embrace,
Chasing each other, what a funny race!
An aloe claims wisdom, smirking in pride,
While spiky succulents just roll and slide.

There's a fern who sways like it's dancing around,
With every bright petal, it spreads joy abound.
The tangle of leaves puts a smile on my face,
In this little haven, there's laughter and grace!

Cacti are cheerleaders, pointy and bright,
Encouraging growth with all of their might.
In this leafy escape, all worries take flight,
Each day feels greener, each moment, pure light!

Silhouettes of the Small

In a miniature world, where shadows play,
Mighty little leaves have much to say.
A moss carpet rolls out like a lush stage,
As earthworms perform in a tiny rage!

Sprouts wave hello, all vibrant and spry,
Each leaf a tale, a question, a sigh.
Little critters peek, thinking they're sly,
But I see the mischief in every small eye!

A droopy geranium feels quite profound,
Wonders if it's the star of this ground.
Basil joins in, with a flourish, a twirl,
Says, "I'm the main dish, give me a whirl!"

In this pot of secrets, laughter abounds,
Where tiny green whispers make joyful sounds.
It's a carnival here, with fun at the core,
Who knew that such chaos could open a door!

The Lush Enclosure

My tiny domain, a forest so bright,
Where plants cast shadows, a whimsical sight.
Each leaf a story, a riddle, a pun,
In the land of the potted, I'm never outdone!

Chia pets chuckle beneath their green curls,
While robust sunflowers toss petals like pearls.
The ferns tell jokes to a sleepy old sprout,
Working together, they figure it out!

A jungle of laughter, where smiles are found,
With each new petal, joy knows no bound.
The herbs conspire on culinary schemes,
In this lush enclosure, we're living in dreams!

As they grow taller, I can't help but cheer,
My indoor adventure, my colorful sphere.
A sanctuary rich with giggles galore,
In this cheerful green haven, who could ask for more?

Nature's Enigma in a Vessel

In a tiny world where greens collide,
A cactus wears a feathered pride.
The ferns do dance with playful glee,
While moss insists it's queen, you see!

A beetle dons a little hat,
While a snail races, oh so flat.
The rocks gossip in ancient tones,
As the painted lady skips on stones.

Air plants hang like graceful swings,
Dropping jokes about their frilly springs.
In this quirky, crowded space,
Nature laughs with a happy face.

A dandelion's dream on display,
Wishes blowing gently away.
In this pot, life's whims unite,
Bringing giggles, pure delight!

Tropics at Your Fingertips

A rubber tree is doing tricks,
While a fern plays hide-and-seek, no fix.
Cacti giggle, sharp but sweet,
A pineapple sports some funky feet.

Chameleons are wearing stripes,
A dance-off with the tiny gripes.
A gossip vine twirls with glee,
While a blob of moss says, 'Look at me!'

A pitcher plant has tea for two,
While orchids wink, look at their hue!
Tiny critters throw a ball,
Playing catch in the mini hall.

In this lush, potted spree,
Laughter echoes, wild and free.
Tropics snug, just out of sight,
Nature's funny little delight!

Hidden Habitat

Beneath the soil, a secret game,
Where tiny bugs are quite the fame.
A ladybug tells ancient myths,
While cricket plays the lute in riffs.

A shy root peeks, curious and meek,
As the ivy laughs, 'Come here, take a peek!'
In this pot, they all convene,
For jokes and pranks that are quite obscene.

Inside a shell, a turtle rests,
Daydreaming of adventurous quests.
The stone's a sage, wise and old,
Sharing tales of the brave and bold.

In this cozy, quirky rest,
Life buzzes on, it's simply the best!
Hidden wonders, jokes in the air,
Nature whispers, 'Isn't this rare?'

Life in a Terrarium

In glassy lands where laughter blooms,
Tiny critters throw boisterous booms.
With leafy hats and wiggly tails,
They race like ships with jittery sails.

A worm with style, quite the fashion,
Snags attention with silly passion.
The beetles knock on glassy doors,
Sipping rain like it's from stores.

In a mini world that's fun to spy,
A dragonfly flutters, oh my!
Beneath the sun, the colors thrive,
Making this pot a playful hive.

Life giggles in every nook,
Nature's pranksters, come take a look!
In this glass, there's never a frown,
Just silly grins all around!

Roots of Exploration

In a tiny vessel, wild things grow,
Mischievous leaves dance to and fro.
A squirrel peeks in, curious and spry,
Wondering if he can fit in this pie.

Tiny vines climb up to the light,
Whispering secrets, such pure delight.
A hidden frog leaps with a splash,
In this small realm, there's quite a clash.

Mice hold a party, all dressed in green,
With acorn hats for a whimsical scene.
They'll toast to their fortune, never alone,
In their pot paradise, feeling at home.

Each root and sprout sings a funny tune,
Under the gaze of a curious moon.
What a mad world created so small,
With laughter and joy, it enthralls us all!

Floral Reverie

Petals keep giggling, colors so bright,
Joking with bees in a mid-afternoon flight.
Daisies wear glasses made out of dew,
Sipping on sunlight, who knew they grew?

A sunflower winks, bold and proud,
While the shy violets huddle, a shy crowd.
A roguish ant steals a sugar cane,
As flowers chuckle, 'The thrill is insane!'

Butterflies dance like they own the spot,
Critiquing their neighbors, all in a plot.
"Watch me flip!" says one, with a zigzag swirl,
In this floral circus, it's a fun-filled whirl.

With petals and laughter, the day drifts away,
In this vibrant life where the blossoms play.
A garden of giggles, pure floral glee,
Bursting with joy, delightful and free!

Spirals of Green Growth

A mischievous snail takes the long route,
On a spiral path where the sprouts salute.
Twisting and twirling, with no end in sight,
He chuckles, "Competition? Not tonight!"

Worms wear their shades, lounging in style,
Keeping a coolness that stretches a mile.
They giggle and squirm under the warm sun,
In this little haven, all critters have fun.

Tiny tomatoes throw a mini parade,
With peppers and radishes, in bright charades.
"Oi, look at us!" they shout in a cheer,
In this pot of mischief, there's nothing to fear.

A whirlwind of greenery, laughter unfolds,
In this jungle of joy where nature beholds.
As sprouts start to giggle in verdant delight,
This vibrant chaos makes everything bright!

The Small World Within

A pebble is king in this pocket of green,
With tiny critters running the scene.
Grassy hats sway in the cheeky breeze,
In their compact kingdom, they aim to please.

A blueberry squawks as it rolls to a stop,
Claiming it rules this great tiny crop.
"Come one, come all!" the mushrooms do call,
For a festivity here that enthralls them all.

Ants wear their boots, marching in rank,
Each step's a giggle, no reason to pranks.
With a tap of a leaf, a dance takes flight,
Under twinkling stars that light up the night.

In this small world, boundaries are few,
Nature's laughter bubbles, bright and true.
From petals to roots, the fun seems to blend,
In the heart of the pot, where joy won't end!

Container of Wonders

In a bowl of soil, a tiny tree,
A gnome pops out, sips his tea.
A snail wears shades, claims it's cool,
While a worm does loops, in endless pool.

Frogs in hats throw a wild dance,
A sunflower winks, takes a chance.
Bees bust out their hip-hop moves,
Nature's party, no one loses!

Tiny ants march, a marching band,
They play with leaves, isn't that grand?
A ladybug sings with delight,
In this pot, all things unite.

Each sprout tells tales of wild dreams,
In this small world, nothing's as it seems.
So grab your spoon, let's dive inside,
For this garden, we laugh with pride!

Verdant Whimsy

A cactus wearing a sparkling crown,
Giggles as raindrops tumble down.
A fern does splits in the pot's embrace,
While a mushroom smiles with a spongy face.

Snakes with ribbons, they dance and sway,
"Come join us!" they call, "What a day!"
Dancing orchids sway left and right,
Pull up a leaf, join the delight!

A bunny hops with a flowery coat,
And tells a joke up on a tote.
Laughter echoes through the green,
In this world of quirky sheen.

With bees that buzz a friendly tune,
And giggles blend with the afternoon.
This pot's alive with joy galore,
Nature's laughter, who could ask for more?

Embrace of the Tentacled Vines

Twisted tendrils reach for the sky,
A potato wants to know why.
"Why do we stretch and sway so wide?"
"Just to see the lawn from inside!"

A carrot hops, "I'm feeling spry!"
While vines whisper, "Look at that guy!"
A tiny lizard, in sun, does pose,
"Welcome to my show! Strike a rose!"

With leaves like umbrellas, they dance along,
To the rhythm of the pot's own song.
"Life's too short for quiet days,
Join the fun, let's all be crazed!"

In this tiny space, light hearts collide,
With every wiggle, smiles abide.
A wild symposium, laughter shared,
In tentacles where no one's scared!

Heart of the Untamed

In a terracotta dome, wildness brews,
Bromeliads gossip, sharing news.
A cactus plans a surprise BBQ,
While a leafy friend sings debut.

A pixie sneezes, and petals quiver,
"Excuse me, I just can't deliver!"
With fireflies twinkling, they all unite,
To spark a party under the night.

The thyme's a jester with a bright green hat,
While chives do backflips, imagine that!
"Join us, dear bugs, let's dance and sing,"
A world in a pot, where joy takes wing.

With colors bright and laughter loud,
In this little realm, they're all so proud.
So sip that nectar, join in the fun,
For our pot's alive, and we've just begun!

Miniature Wilderness

A tiny world, so loud and bright,
Butterflies dance, quite the sight.
A gnome with shades, lounging in a chair,
In this mini wild, without a care.

Tiny vines creep up the wall,
A tree so small, yet standing tall.
The critters joke, it's quite a show,
Who knew a pot could steal the glow?

The mushrooms wear their polka dots,
While squirrels trade their thimble knots.
A ladybug rules with a tiny crown,
In this pot, there's never a frown.

Watch out for the sneaky beetle's chase,
In this vibrant, playful space.
When rain falls, it's a little splash,
A garden party, oh what a bash!

Verdant Dreams in Clay

In a flowerpot, dreams take flight,
Where ants journey all day and night.
A snail with style, his shell so chic,
Whispers jokes, oh so unique.

The herbs all giggle, tickled by breeze,
As petals debate who'll win 'Best Freeze'.
A lizard struts on a twiggy stage,
In this pot, everyone's the sage.

A raindrop's a pool, a splashdown fun,
Where grasshoppers leap, oh what a run!
The daisies dance, oh what a spree,
This patch isn't just for you or me.

With each new sprout, laughter spreads wide,
In this glorious green, we all abide.
Frogs sing tunes from atop the stones,
In this clay realm, we're never alone!

The Enclosed Wild

Sky-high grasses, so much to scale,
In a pot, we tell a wild tale.
The critters giggle, in shades of green,
Plotting escapades rarely seen.

A butterfly grins, lands with flair,
While the cactus tries to comb its hair.
A pipe-cleaner creature joins the fun,
In this brave new world, all are one.

Watch as mushrooms launch a dance,
While a tiny toad gives it a chance.
The soil is rich with laughter's thread,
In this closed wild, no tears are shed.

A roly-poly rolls, just for laughs,
While the sunbeams become clever drafts.
In this pot of dreams, we're all so spry,
The enclosed wild, oh my, oh my!

Urban Eden

Nestled in concrete, a green delight,
Where plants and laughter bloom, oh what a sight!
Tiny turtles wear their shades of cool,
While squirrels dive into a pool.

A cactus throws a spiky party,
Inviting all, both grumpy and hearty.
The tomatoes giggle, red cheeks abound,
In this urban realm, silliness is found.

Neighborhood bees buzz tunes so sweet,
There's always a dance-off down the street.
The sunflowers sway, with hats on their heads,
In this playful patch, no one dreads.

With rain clouds looming, it's no big fuss,
The drizzles come, and we all discuss.
In this pot, we're living the dream,
In an urban paradise, or so it seems!

Verdant Whirls of Life

In a bowl of soil, plants do dance,
Tiny leaves twirl, in a leafy trance.
A pepper plant dreams of spicy sights,
While daisies gossip about their heights.

Worms play tag in the rich black clay,
"Who's the fastest?" they giggle and sway.
The basil dreams of faraway lands,
While thyme wraps its arms around all its fans.

A cactus grins, with spikes so bold,
"I'm the tough one, or so I'm told!"
Yet here we laugh, in our cozy space,
Where every sprout wears a charming face.

The pot's alive, with giggles and cheers,
Each leaf a story, taking on fears.
In this little world, let the fun ignite,
Where roots and laughter mingle all night.

Serenity in a Shallow Nest

In a little cup, a fern does sway,
Thinking it's grown, come what may.
"A tree!" it shouts, "on my leafy throne!"
While crickets chirp in playful tone.

A miniature jungle, how it blooms,
Potting soil hides all the funny grooms.
Tiny bugs, like mates, take a stroll,
Each one ready to play a role.

A sunflower dreams of a tall parade,
"Look at me! I'm a big charade!"
While succulents giggle in hues so bright,
"Oh, we're just cozy, out of sight!"

A parakeet swings, thinking it's grand,
In a pot full of treasures, a bright wonderland.
No jungle too wild, no leaf too small,
In this shallow nest, there's room for all.

Fables of the Green Thumb

Once a seedling wished on a starry night,
"I'll grow so tall; oh, what a sight!"
But out popped a sprout, short and round,
"It seems I'm stuck, in my little mound."

A ladybug laughed, "You're quite a find,
In this pot of dreams, the fun's not blind!"
"Let's throw a party," the herbs all agreed,
With potpourri scents, they danced with speed.

"Chlorophyll's my color, green's my game,"
Chanted a leaf with flair and fame.
We'll swap our tales of mischief and cheer,
In this quirky patch, we've nothing to fear!

So here we grow, in our little domain,
Where laughter and green mix up the grain.
Every sprout whispers secrets loud,
In this whimsical pot, we're all so proud.

Earth's Embrace in a Sphere

In a roundy pot, all snug and tight,
Lives a fat bulb who loves the night.
Gossiping roots, they weave a tale,
Of giggles and dreams that never pale.

Cacti and ferns share garden space,
With quirky tricks and a cheerful face.
"Who can grow the biggest leaf?" they ask,
While climbing vines take on the task.

A tiny gnome guards the flowers' bloom,
With a goofy grin as he clears the room.
"Stand back, I'll show my greenest tricks!"
As petals burst forth in a funny mix.

In this sphere of life, joy leaps and spins,
Where weeds are heroes and chaos wins.
With every chuckle and leafy surprise,
In this merry pot, our laughter flies.

www.ingramcontent.com/pod-product-compliance
Lightning Source LLC
Chambersburg PA
CBHW070318120526
44590CB00017B/2733